Dedication:
"For Hupáhu and all future generations, may they soar high on spiritual wings to meet the dawning of a new day."

ISBN: 978-1-9891222-2-8
Printed in PRC
Published in Canada by Medicine Wheel Publishing
For more book information go to https://medicinewheelpublishing.com

Medicine Wheel Publishing

The Eagle Feather

The Eagle Feather is an adaptation of the book **Dawn Flight: A Lakota Story**, by Kevin Locke, for a younger audience (ages 4-6). For the purpose of connecting with this age group, Kevin's beautiful story was simplified to focus on what the eagle represents to him (courage, honesty and kindness) and how we can all learn from the eagle. This adaptation has been created with Kevin Locke and has his enthusiastic approval. We are excited to share it with you.

Look! Up there — an eagle flying by.
Let's follow his journey as he soars through the sky!

This beautiful eagle can teach us many things,
he has as many lessons as feathers on his wings.

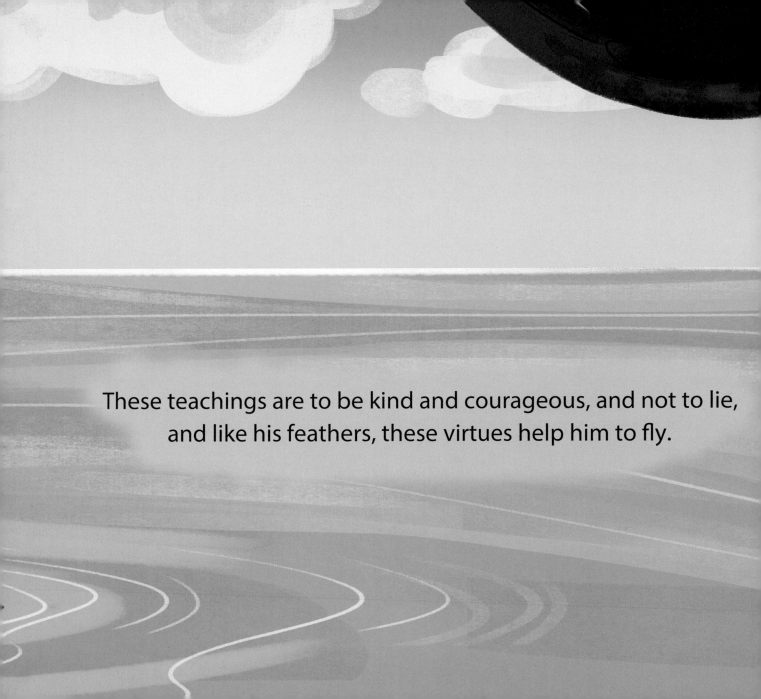

These teachings are to be kind and courageous, and not to lie, and like his feathers, these virtues help him to fly.

I recognize the spirit of the eagle in myself and in you.
We must fly towards the light in all that we do!

Hey, look at what I have found!
An eagle feather floating to the ground.

Little one! What a blessing this is!
The eagle wanted you to have something that was his.

Find the eagle in yourself and others, day and night,
and you can soar above darkness, into the light.

Remember this story
and you'll know what to do.
You can share the eagle's lessons
with friends and family too.

A few words in Lakota

čhaŋwákhaŋ: the Great Tree of Life

tȟuŋkášila: the Grandfather above

waŋblí : eagle

wíyaka: feather

About the Author

Kevin Locke is a world-renowned Hoop Dancer, distinguished Indigenous Northern Plains flutist, traditional storyteller, cultural ambassador, recording artist, and educator. Kevin is Lakota (from the Hunkpapa Band of the Lakota Sioux), and Anishinabe. His Lakota name is Tȟokéya Ináźiŋ, meaning "First to Arise." Kevin Locke presents and performs at hundreds of performing arts centers, festivals, schools, universities, conferences, state and national parks, monuments, historic sites, powwows, and reservations every year. Approximately eighty percent of these are shared with children. Kevin is a dance and musical hero and role model for youth around the world. His special joy is working with children on reservations to ensure the survival and growth of Indigenous culture.

Kevin Locke is a world famous performer and educator with over 30 years of experience. He shares an educational and engaging message of unity, peace, culture and history in all of his performances and school programs.

Find more of Kevin's school programs through the Online Education Curriculum of the Patricia Locke Foundation. This includes:

- Reading, Writing & Comprehension Using Indigenous Stories.
- K-12 program comprising audio and visual materials by Kevin Locke.
- Dance, storytelling, and music; bringing lessons to life.
- Indigenous language incorporated into the educational materials, with English translation.
- Companion materials including Teacher's Guides, Lesson Plans and Student Activity Sheets.

To learn more, visit:
patricialockefoundation.org
kevinlocke.com

BEYOND
THE ORANGE
SHIRT STORY

Phyllis Webstad

A collection of stories from family and friends of
Phyllis Webstad before, during, and after their
Residential School experiences.

ORANGE SHIRT DAY
SEPTEMBER 30TH

Orange Shirt Society

Edited and Approved by
Phyllis Webstad & Joan Sorley

The Eagle Feather

Written By Kevin Locke
Illustrated by Jessika von Innerebner

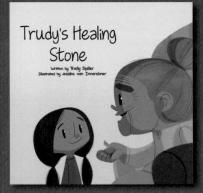

Trudy's Healing Stone

Written by Trudy Spiller
Illustrated by Jessika von Innerebner

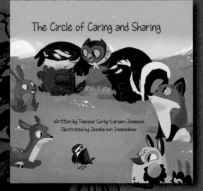

The Circle of Caring and Sharing

Written by Theresa 'Corky' Larsen-Jonasson
Illustrated by Jessika von Innerebner

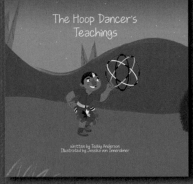

The Hoop Dancer's Teachings

Written by Teddy Anderson
Illustrated by Jessika von Innerebner

Phyllis's Orange Shirt

Written by Phyllis Webstad
Illustrated by Brock Nicol

Gifts from Raven

Written by Kung Jaadee
Illustrated by Jessika von Innerebner

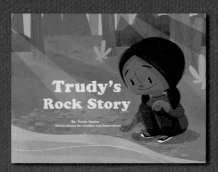

Trudy's
Rock Story

By: Trudy Spiller
Illustrations by: Jessika von Innerebner

The Orange Shirt Story

Author: Phyllis Webstad
Illustrations: Brock Nicol

The
SHARING
CIRCLE

WRITTEN BY
Theresa "Corky" Larsen-Jonasson

ILLUSTRATED BY
Jessika von Innerebner

RAVEN'S
FEAST

BY Kung Jaadee

ILLUSTRATED BY Jessika von Innerebner

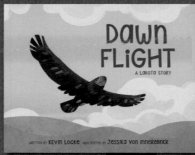

DAWN
FLIGHT
A Lakota Story

WRITTEN BY Kevin Locke   ILLUSTRATED BY Jessika von Innerebner

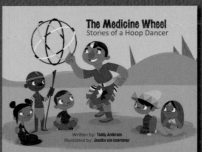

The Medicine Wheel
Stories of a Hoop Dancer

Written by: Teddy Anderson
Illustrated by: Jessika von Innerebner

THIS IS WHAT
I'VE BEEN TOLD
MII YI GAA-KI-WIINDMAAGOOYAAN

WRITTEN & ILLUSTRATED BY
Deborah Armstrong

Meet Your
Family
Gikenim Giniigi'igoog

David Bouchard

We Learn
From the
Sun

David Bouchard
Paintings by Kristy Cameron

Visit our online store at:
medicinewheelpublishing.com